ADVANCE PRAISE

Silverman's stories are moving and his life solutions are innovative and powerful.

I highly recommend this book!!!

STEVE CHANDLER AUTHOR OF *CRAZY GOOD*

Mark Silverman is gifted with bottom-line honesty, which shines through this short but potent book. If you can grasp even a portion of Mark's sense of pointed intention, you will be well ahead of where you stood before. Mark is devoted to living at the frequency of purpose, and he would love to have you meet him there. Don't hesitate to fly.

ALAN COHEN AUTHOR OF *A DEEP BREATH OF LIFE*

Mark's idea of living life by following only your 10 out of 10s is a game changer. It transcends the latest fads in time-management, online scheduling or planning apps. It also moves beyond complex systems like David Allen's Getting Things Done or Steven Covey's Four Quadrants.

Warren Buffett once said, "The difference between successful people and really successful people is that really successful people say no to almost everything." The only problem is how do you know what to say no to?

If you are overwhelmed by never-ending to do lists, Only 10s will help you cut straight to the heart of time and life management. And it gives you a road map for when to say Hell Yeah and when to say Hell No.

Only 10's is a must read for entrepreneurs, executives, leaders and innovators.

RICH LITVIN CO-AUTHOR OF *THE PROSPEROUS COACH/* FOUNDER OF 4PC

Mark is first and foremost an incredible human being, friend and a dedicated coach; he's highly intentional and he makes things happen when he says he will — for himself and for others. And as he points out in this new book, he's also learned the fine art of prioritization. It's the key to making the most important things happen in your life. If it's not a "hell yes" for now, then it's a "hell no." As you learn to slow down and trust your gut, you too will be able to sift the 10's out of the pile — jettison the rest — and watch your productivity and fulfillment soar. Mark outlines the techniques he uses which have been proven to work for him; give them a try and thrive!

KELLI RICHARDS CEO, ALL ACCESS GROUP

ONLY 10s

USING DISTRACTION TO GET THE RIGHT THINGS DONE

MARK J. SILVERMAN

COPYRIGHT

DISCLAIMER

Cover Design: John Matthews

Interior Design: Heidi Miller

Editing: Kate Makled & Grace Kerina

Author's photo courtesy of Rebecca Biddle Moseman

DEDICATION

For my family: John, Robin, Zack and Jake.

You are my 10s, my True North, and the reason
life is so freakin' awesome.

TABLE OF CONTENTS

INTRODUCTION

Maybe, like me, you have attended the seminars, bought the tools, practiced the principles and still failed to finally "get organized," once and for all. If so, I'm sure you wondered, "How the hell can an intelligent, educated, successful person be so miserably inadequate at writing out a list of tasks and then accomplishing said tasks?" Perhaps we are kindred spirits.

I had a beautiful leather bound Franklin Planner. I prioritized A, B, C items. I forwarded my list from day to day. I worked on Big Rocks and let go of the small ones. For about 2 days.

I spent $1,500 and an entire day learning the "Getting Things Done" program. I love that program, and that system. I spent days listing everything, I bought a label maker to make my files clear, organized and attractive. I touched nothing more than once. That lasted about a week.

Six months later, I took the refresher class, and reset once again. I got three days out of it that time.

The irony of my story is that I was a top salesman in the fast-paced and highly competitive IT world for 15 years. I won awards year after year, and earned millions. However, I felt constantly overwhelmed. I felt like a fraud. Every situation was a last minute buzzer beater. I loved the adrenaline rush of being the hero that saved the quarter, but hated the stress and fear that came with the self imposed job description.

Unfortunately, I knew no other way. No matter what I did, I could not become "organized, methodical, deliberate." It was almost impossible to set a plan, follow the steps and "execute." Except at the last minute. When everything focused down, the deadline was looming and it was clear what needed to be done, I could block everything else out, blow through any barrier, and close the sale.

Fear drove me every day. Fear of failure, fear of being found out. Adrenaline saved me at the last minute, over and over again. Fog and confusion were my constant companions, which I learned later was undiagnosed A.D.D. Glad to have the label, Adderall and Ritalin helped quite a bit, but only if I decided what to work on and sat myself down to do so.

I didn't know it at the time, but there was a clue in that last minute buzzer beater ability to focus. Why am I great in a crisis? Why, when I decide I want a new car in the morning, can I have one in my driveway by that very evening? Why can my son (also diagnosed with A.D.D.) sit down and figure out the new Verizon Fios menus and remote, but struggle with an English paper? Why does he know every baseball player, their stats and where they are from? "Mark, it's not true you can't focus. When you are excited by something, I've seen you focus and accomplish amazing things," my coach, Rich Litvin, said to me one day.

It's absolutely true that when I am interested in something, I can focus. When my son wants a goal, nothing will stop him. When it is a 10 on a scale of 1–10, something miraculous happens. It gets done. No tools, programs or seminars. It just gets done.

So here you are. You've picked up yet another book on "Time (please help me get organized) Management," or self-management, or getting things done — in hopes of some new method or insight that might flip a switch. Maybe this book will finally get you to hunker down and do what you know you should be doing. This isn't that book!

What you have here are my notes and experiences of what happened after I realized that I actually do focus... when I give a shit. And I don't...when I don't. I can share with you that once I let go and started trusting this "inner compass," amazing things happened. Time opened up, more and more got done, and I learned that I can trust myself to focus on what needs to be focused on most. I learned that this inner guidance of following what excites me, actually got my taxes done, insurance papers submitted, and an entire book written.

This discovery has worked a miracle in my life. I get stuff done. I get stuff done that is important to me. I can now trust myself to follow through on a large goal or vision because I have found my "why," and "want to," that is essential for me to actually care and focus.

As I discovered this new way of looking at the world, my life and business began to open up. I shared my insights with clients who also had big goals...and big distractions. As we went through their "to do" lists, their eyes opened to the internal compass approach, and they too dropped the dead weight that made each day more difficult than it needed to be. They learned to trust themselves, and in turn found the energy to move forward on creative endeavors, creating whole new divisions and projects to move their businesses forward.

MY STORY

WHAT IT WAS LIKE

I'd review my agenda each morning, diligently and clear-eyed:

Big plans today! I know just who to call, and I have an idea for a marketing blitz. I really need to get the sales forecast done for my boss. It is due in 3 days, but if I start now, I can get all the info together. I have presentations at 10 and 2PM, and hopefully I can squeeze a haircut in afterward. I need to call my mom, and I want to check on my friend who had back surgery. Oh shoot, I need to get Jake to his baseball game by 5:30. OK, I got it — if I just stay on track.

As the day goes on, so does the internal dialog:

So much to do today. I am overwhelmed. How am I going to get it all done? If I were just more organized. If I were more disciplined. I'm capable of so much more. If I were firing on all cylinders, I'd be freaking rich! If they knew how much I didn't get done, I'd get fired! I know I met my goals this month, but what the heck am I going to do next month? I can't keep this up. I need a break. Why is everyone always asking me for stuff. Why can't I get any help?

I was exhausted before I started. Every day felt like a treadmill on full speed and if I stopped for a minute, I would fall off the back. Every Monday — er, even Sunday night — was full of anxiety. No matter how successful I was, the feeling of being a fraud was a constant. The "to do" list got longer and longer and most of the time, it seemed I was working on anything but that list.

In my head I longed for relief. Relief looked like being fired, or getting sick...really anything to stop the madness. Resentment was a constant, because the world asked too damn much of me. Yes, I'll pick that up. Yes, I can get that to you, No I don't need help...I'm fine. You would think my name was "Earnest."

To add to the constant worry about being all things to all people, I wondered to myself, why I seemingly had to work three times as hard to get half as much done. Why did I feel lazy even though I never stopped? Why did I feel like I was using ten percent of my capacity? I was diagnosed with A.D.D. in my 40s. It was a relief to know there was a reason for my scattered path to every destination, but it still didn't change that fact. Ritalin was a fantastic tool. I could take it, and then if I could get myself to start a project, I could get 2 hours of good solid work done. The trick was to send the ship in the right direction, or even *that* tool did not work for me.

I was constantly plagued with the thought, "Why can't I keep my word to myself?" I want to be the kind of person who says they will do something, then does it. Discipline. I need discipline. If I just had more discipline. The self-judgment and shame followed me everywhere.

Of course I purchased a Franklin Planner and did the workshop. Several times. The "Getting Things Done" Program was a lifesaver. For a week. I worked on habits, big goals, little goals, chunking, aromatherapy, music therapy (actually that worked as well as the Ritalin for projects I actually got started). Half of my time was spent working on the tools to get me to get to the work that needed to get done. I seemingly single handedly supported the multimillion-dollar Time Management/Productivity industry, and would have gladly continued.

WHAT HAPPENED?

One day, I was whining to my coach, "This A.D.D. is kicking my ass! I have focused down to five projects that are really important to me, I take my Ritalin, cleared the decks, and I still can't get my work done. It is driving me crazy!"

He said, "Mark, what if you used the A.D.D. and resistance as a compass instead of a problem? What if you trusted your attention and your energy to take you where you need to go?"

To which I replied, "Then I would be homeless, my kids would go hungry, and everything would fall apart."

But I was intrigued. Excited even. The problem was, I had this internal belief that if I gave myself slack, or trusted where my attention went as a *priority* system, I wouldn't be motivated to do anything but eat and binge on Netflix. Trust myself? Not a chance.

He asked me to humor him, and we went through my projects one by one. For each one, we tested my commitment to the goals and needs of each project. In Rich's language, life's opportunities were either a "Hell Yes" or a "Hell No." I have described myself as a person with an On and an Off switch, though I fight it every step of the way. We used the scale of 1–10 to evaluate my list. They landed as follows.

Project 1) No question, I loved this one, it holds a ton of juice for me. This is a Hell Yes. A 10.

Project 2) This is my lifeblood. It is my business and the reason I do this work. Absolutely a 10.

Project 3) Very important to me, I want to do this. I love working with these people. I can't seem to get to it. I don't want to disappoint anyone though, I committed to it...Oh shit, this isn't a 10. It's more like a 9. No wonder I can't get to it.

Project 4) This one has to happen. I cannot delegate, the ball is rolling and the deadline coming. I will *not* let these people down. Boom, a 10.

Project 5) I get the game by now. No, this is a "should." I don't really want to do it but it seems crazy not to. A 5 at best.

I was left with three projects that, according to my internal compass, were filled with energy and motivation. Dropping the other two came with fear because I needed to have honest conversations about my not really wanting to do them. I hate disappointing people I love and respect (and want to like me). I had my 10s.

And then I had my *Aha!* moment. I thought back to when I ran the Marine Corps Marathon a few years ago.

My marriage had ended and my career was on the express elevator to the basement. I was having panic attacks, and got very sick, weakening my body and adding to my depression. As my health came back, and I got a new job, I wanted my kids to see how their Dad handled adversity. I needed something crazy to snap me back. In hindsight, I needed a 10.

I was listening to the radio, while waiting for another doctor appointment, when I heard Dr. Oz interviewing some "crazy" ultra marathon guy...at least from my vantage point, ultra-marathoning seemed a little crazy. He talked about green drinks, alkalizing, and he believed that everyone could run, *everyone*. Bad knees, no muscle mass, bad back...I can run? I absolutely will grab on to the craziest things!

I got his book, devoured it, and started the painful walk/run of 1 mile per day. Then 2. Then 3 miles of slow jogging while filling my head with self help books and audios of every flavor. A special shout out to Brian Johnson's Philosopher's Notes, for getting me through mile after mile. I made a decision. It was early March and against all good advice, I signed up for the 26.2 Mile Marine Corps Marathon. I told everyone who would listen, and I raised thousands of dollars for charity, so there was no backing out. The impossible happened, I ran the Marine Corps Marathon with only eight months of running experience, let alone training, because it was a 10.

My 10 looks like it was the marathon itself, but in actuality, it was deeper than that. The real, driving, 10 was my kids — and the influence I had on them. The MCM was my task. A difficult, resistance-filled task at that. An added 10 was in saving face. By raising all that money and being so public about my objective, I used my inner fear of looking bad to motivate me. Since not looking bad was a 10, for me, sore knees became a 9.5.

How do I know the MCM was a 10 for me? Because I did it. And it was this clue that that tipped my hand when Rich said to me, "Mark, nothing stops you when you really want to do something. A.D.D. is not an issue, resistance isn't an issue, fear isn't even an issue. You just do it."

He was right. I couldn't believe it. Half the stuff on my "to-do" list had qualifiers. I should do this. I am afraid of not doing this. What will people think if I say no? Once I addressed the qualifiers, I got clear on what I wanted to do and what I did not want to do. It was getting harder to lie to myself.

The conversation and realization exposed the "victim" mentality I lived with, the one I imposed on myself. Nobody was making me do anything, I was *choosing* to do everything I did, and mainly because the choice of *not* doing it was something I wanted to avoid. Consequences had been dictating my 10s, nobody was "making" me do anything. I would choose to *not* do something I really wanted to do, because I wanted to avoid some pain or fear. I was always choosing. I let that sink in for a moment. I'm still letting it sink in. I always do 10s, my reasons for declaring something a 10 (or intuitively gravitating to it as such) just may not be apparent at first. More on this later.

WHAT IT'S LIKE NOW

I still have A.D.D. I still get easily distracted. I still rebel, resist, and I would much rather read a juicy news article than do my work. What's changed? Everything!

By pausing for a moment and considering each task on my plate, or new request coming my way, I can consider my inner compass, and discern the motive for choosing whether or not to I take it on. My thought process revolves around an internal flow chart with intersections consisting of various questions. Do I want to or not? Am I avoiding something unpleasant or is fear influencing my choice? Is there a "should" anywhere in the equation? If there is resistance, what is that about? Do I have beliefs, real or imagined, that have undue influence over this decision? Are they true?

Once I ferret out these "qualifiers," everything changes. I feel freedom, I can think, and my perception of life slows down. I can hear my own inner voice of preference. I am clear about what I want to do and don't want to do. The process of deciding what to do with my time has slowed down, so I can navigate all the inputs that go into making decisions, giving me the choice over responding to outside influences. Mostly, I am happy — for no reason — a lot more of the time.

More specifically, keeping the above in mind, I get more done. My to-do list gets done (completely!) almost every day. It is much shorter, much more focused list, but it all gets done. I end the day with energy and a sense of forward progress. If it goes on my list, I can trust myself to get it done. If I have resistance to a task, I have the energy and willingness to get past it. That, in and of itself, is a miracle.

The only discipline I really need is to slow down and pay attention so I can make a choice. For the first time in my life, I feel like I have moved from Potential to Action.

WHAT IS A 10?

10!

Hell Yes!

All In!

A "10" is a "Hell Yes." It is an *all in, nothing is going to stop me, I want this more than anything* kind of feeling. You will know it is a 10 because you are doing it now, or you're clear that nothing or no one can stop you from doing it. Think about that *one thing* you did that seemed crazy or impossible and you did it anyway. There are very few true 10s. But once you look, they are clear. Once you see them, it ruins your 9's forever, not to mention the 8s and 7s. The Marine

Corps Marathon shattered my illusion and showed me exactly who I am, and what I am capable of, *when I want to do something.*

We can categorize 10s in several ways. While they support each other, it is not essential to build an entire interlocking system. I have found, by being conscious of all the ways a 10 fits into my life, I easily become conscious of the natural interconnectedness they share.

The three categories worth our attention are Big Picture 10s, more immediate (or this week's) 10s and — front and center — today's 10s. In the original exercise with Rich, we clarified my Big 10s by examining my goals and visions. When I start a week, I clear the decks and decide what I really want to have happen this week. Most importantly, I care about what is happening right in front of me. Today. This moment.

Let's start with today's 10s.

Today's 10s
You really want to do it.
Deadline, due date or consequence if not done today.
Anything scheduled.

My morning clients will often start our session with "I am so overwhelmed, I do not know how I am going to get it all done." So I slow them down, and have them write down today's list. Here's an example.

Today's List
8am Mark
9:30am Vendor Meeting
11 AM VP meeting
Two offer letters
2PM Interview
Book CA trip
Backfill Network Admin
Assisted living for my mom
Email
Presentation for all hands
I want to get to the gym
Back to school night for Kid

First, we go through the appointments scheduled, then on to the tasks crowding the plate. We question each item on the list and, one by one, put each through its own paces. Is each meeting necessary for him to attend? If it is going to be on the list, it needs to fight to get there.

In the example, the two offer letters are for quality candidates waiting to come aboard and fill open positions that, left empty, are burying him and his team. They stay. The

California trip isn't for 3 weeks yet, so it is not a 10 for today and it can wait. He still may book his trip today, but it takes no room on the "must happen, will do, no questions," list. Backfilling the Network admin is a project — and the only active action item is to send a job description to personnel. He desperately needs that position filled, so an action toward that happening is a 10 for today. He realizes he could ask his brother to gather four websites for places for their mom, so we decide this is another project and just a single action item gets the 10 for today, and it's reduced to a quick email. The all-hands meeting is tomorrow, and that presentation needs to be done today if being prepared is a 10. The presentation itself is not a 10, it is the outcome of the presentation that needs to have the energy to pull him through the task. Seeing himself successful on stage creates an excitement and a want for the project. He missed his window for going to the gym. It will not happen in the afternoon today (if we tell the truth about it), and consequently it comes off the list. If the gym is really a 10, he will be there tomorrow morning. Email is never a 10. It fills in the gaps. A response to an email can possibly be a 10, but it must be treated like Facebook and the news.

A 10 must get done today, for a real reason, and must be done by me.

The new list of Today's 10s for this client looks like this:

Today's List
- ✓ 8am Mark
- 9:30am Vendor Meeting
- 11 AM VP meeting
- Two offer letters
- 2PM Interview
- Job description to HR
- Ask Fred to search 4 places for mom.
- Presentation for all hands
- Back to school night for Kid

What changed in his day? The meetings were deemed important. The meeting with me is done, so it gets a check. The failure of not going to the gym is eliminated, and no longer takes up space on the list, nor in his head. Two in-depth items are now reduced to the absolutely essential five minute tasks to move major projects forward (Description to HR and Note to brother), so a couple of heavy projects no longer crowd the daily field and overwhelm him. He now knows that even email takes a back seat to the presentation tomorrow. He has the room to make an impact on stage the next day. His kid is a 10, so he will be at the school — and with this focus and confidence that he did the right things today, in a better mood to enjoy being a Dad.

Can you feel some breathing room? A little less tension? Yeah, but.

But what about interruptions? The email needs to get done, people expect answers. Yes, they do. This is where the work comes in. *This is where I learned the most about myself, and my ability to prioritize my day.* If I got into a car accident, I would not be available for last minute interruptions and I wouldn't be on email. The decision is made *for* me because something unavoidable came up. It miraculously prioritizes my life. Action item one, stop the bleeding. Our 10s need to have that level of urgency, and we cannot fabricate that level of focus. We must find it in order to make sure it gets done, because we decided it was the right, most important thing to get done.

If the two offer letters and the presentation are truly 10s, if they will make the biggest impact in my client's life, then they are as important as a car accident. If he can blow off the presentation and wing it on stage, or let the offer letters slide, then they were not a 10 to begin with — and did not belong on the list for that reason.

10s are the "if I only got this one thing done today, it would be a great day" kind of things.

I repeat, if you can let it slide, plan to maybe let it slide, or won't fight for it, it is not a true 10 and does not belong on your list. Learn to be honest with yourself. You can still do it, put it on the list, but be honest — that other things truly do take precedence — so tomorrow you have a little more awareness when making your choices.

Sometimes the 10 list is one thing. Just one. I tell my client that they can be interrupted all day, do email, read Facebook — but if there is an item on the to-do list that is a 10, if they can get that one item completed and it changes everything — do it. Then don't worry about the rest of the day.

Warning: 10s are addictive. Once you find out you can defend your time, and feel the freedom, you will go back for more. Facebook does become irritating.

As with everything worthwhile, this is a practice. I learned more about myself, and I can learn more about the deep inner workings of any client, just by going through a to-do list. Stay with this experiment and within 3 days you will start to see a shift. Even if you quit, nothing will be the same.

Let's go bigger.

How do I know what I want to do each day? I mostly follow my excitement and energy, trusting that the flow will lead to more goodness than my past fighting and struggling ever did. Although I follow this intuitive path, I give it direction by using a compass. I ground myself in a well-vetted list of projects, my 10s, that are deeply meaningful to me. The desire to work on them overcomes my desires for shorter-term "cool stuff" that inevitably vies for my attention.

Shiny objects lose their luster when the pot of gold shines just as bright.

First, two quick stories that led to a complete reshuffling of my priorities and added needed focus and enthusiasm.

Warren Buffet was having a conversation with one of his staff, and asked him to write down 25 things that he really wanted to accomplish this year. After the list was done, Mr. Buffet asked him to identify the top 5 that he really wanted to focus on. The man presented the list and Mr. Buffet asked, "When will you work on the other 20?" The man answered, "Whenever I can find the time and I am not working on the 5."

"NO!" said Mr. Buffett, "You avoid those other 20 like poison."

Focus...and vehement boundaries! I had those five items on my list when I had my conversation with my coach, Rich. Turns out two of those items were not 10s and so they did not belong in the top 5. Dropping those two freed me up to focus even more, because I recovered the energy and focus from the work I was doing toward them — and even more because the focus came back from the fear, anxiety and guilt I felt when they were still on my list — but I wasn't doing anything toward them!

Mark Zuckerberg of Facebook is famous for being manically focused on his company having One Goal: Grow Facebook. *Every idea, every project his team brought to the table, he would ask, "Does it help us grow?" If it didn't fit into that one area of focus, it was taken off the table.*

That got me thinking about Warren Buffet's Top 5, or for me, Top 3 Focus areas. If the smartest and most successful people drive towards one goal, what is mine? If I use my language, what is my ultimate 10? Do I even have a single 10?

I thought about recent conversations with my clients, and found some interesting observations. Some had a clear goal or vision already. They knew what they wanted to build, so we were able to work backwards from that set point to determine which projects would be 10s in that context. Others did not have an ultimate goal and were searching. These were my "explorers," the clients who have finally allowed themselves to think outside the box of their existing busy lives and careers, and look at more possibilities. With these clients, we focused on values, current projects, and energy inventories (listing items that give energy and items that drain) to start to form that "one place" on the map to strive for. Often it was a direction without a destination, but it was a clear direction.

I call it the *compass*. True north is necessary to identify, and keeps us from straying too far off the path wherever we may go. I fell in love with this process of clarifying life's direction, and I saw it add rocket fuel to my client's lives, so I will dedicate a chapter to helping you find your own true north later in this book (Finding True North).

FALSE 1Os

Earnestness

Netflix

False Beliefs

Shiny Objects

Fear

Facebook

9.9s

Addictions

Should

Boundaries

News

Juicy

Looking Good

Other People's 1Os

Because I can

So many things feel like a 10, but absolutely aren't. Some are obvious like Facebook, and the news (online, TV or otherwise). They suck me in, with their juicy and enticing headlines. Marketers (and friends) know everything I want from a 10: a quick hit, a distraction, an emotional response, anything to get that dopamine going instead of whatever "task" I am doing now. They are clearly not 10s, in hindsight, but they are still tempting. I'm sure you have your own false 10s that are actually distractions. But they acted like a 10, maybe because you were interested in doing them, and they also implied priority by holding up a sign saying, essentially, "I'm a 10." Again, marketers, headline writers, and a whole lot of people know how to write enticing headlines and pitches to get us to believe the choice to engage with their content, product or service is our next 10.

False 10s steal the only things I really own, my time and attention.

Addictions are false 10s that actually drive our entire lives. The relief from an uncomfortable feeling, or a difficult task, is the 10. We are like lab rats, every day, looking for quick hits of comfort. This can come from something as benign as a cookie here and there, or lead to the devastation of alcoholism. I lump the seemingly harmless and the life threatening together to illustrate a point, but I do not take either of them lightly.

Addictions do not fight fair, and I have no illusion that this program will alleviate what has baffled man for centuries. If addiction is kicking your ass, I strongly encourage you to seek help. I know that territory and the life beyond it. As of now, 25 years sober, I implore you to do so.

That said, finding recovery after hitting a bottom from an addiction is when living becomes the 10, even as the addiction unfairly fights as a 9.9 with dirty tactics.

The equation still applies. Whatever we use habitually to relieve ourselves from our feelings, fears and pain becomes the 10 once addicted, and keeps us from even the most earnest of pursuits. In AA, they say, "think the drink through," meaning anticipate the consequences to the end. Though recovery involves quite a bit more than intellectual curiosity, the exercise can often unlock the hold it has on us, if we simply and firstly interrupt the impulse. I can honestly say, I have been addicted to news, and particularly the heated arguments that come from political debates. I would much rather have a passionate argument, feel the outrage, and be "right" than focus on monotonous and low-passion necessities like paying my bills. But it's a trap. It's a distraction, and I do not want it taking me away from my 10s, from my own life.

Other people's 10s are not my 10s, unless I choose them to be, but then they *are* mine.
Other people's priorities are false 10s that we make our own. It is a 10 for us, because we want to please. Of course, it can be a 10 if we really want to help someone, but I am talking about the times when we do it for other reasons. Pleasing, being a good guy, invoking our alter ego named "Earnest," or simply not dealing with the annoyance of the asker is actually the 10, not the task itself.

If you have ever had a coworker adept at the "cold bristle manipulation," perhaps you know what I mean. "Oh, I'll just take care of it instead of dealing with Herb's wrath," means that avoiding Herb's tantrum is the 10, while doing what you wanted to do is the 9.

If I catch myself thinking "I should do this," I stop.

I have a few alarms in my head. When I hear myself say "I should do this," I immediately stop. I ask more questions. "Why *should* I do this? Do I want to do this?" If it needs to be done, needs to be done now and by me, I find out why, and I make that my 10. It only gets to be a 10 if it passes the internal interrogation.

Meet Earnest

Earnest is my alter ego. The carrier of false 10s. My nicer, harder working, "always there for people" other self. It's not that I am not a kind or helpful person, its just that Earnest likes to make me look and feel bad. Earnest will say "yes" to every project, every committee. Earnest will stop at the store, take on the extra work, stay late so you can go home, and apologize for not doing enough. Earnest will hide being tired and stretched too thin, his resentments, and even his opinions, if they will cause others to be uncomfortable.

Earnest is too polite, too useful, and a joy to everyone who meets him.

But Earnest is a nightmare for 10s. He will give them up in a heart beat. Earnest is the nicest, most benign, yet deadliest enemy you will ever meet. He will give away your precious time and attention, and stop you from asking for help.

He will kill your focus, your energy, your progress, and maybe even compromise your health.

Beware of Earnest.

I am amazed at the amount of time and life that fear has stolen from me.

Fear is my other alarm bell. It used to be that I would skip over the fear and go right to the task (or avoid the task) without noticing that sneaky motivation. I didn't notice my life getting smaller and smaller because of all my little daily fears. Now I can slow it all down enough — my racing thoughts and my overwhelming feelings — to feel the fear, understand its roots, and decide.

Over time, fear gets easier to spot, so I can master the art of leaning into what I fear. The fear of disappointing someone, fear of looking bad if I say no, fear of being left out, or fear of other people's beliefs, all buffet me about. I really want to get up to dance, but I don't want to be the first one up there. I will email that customer 12 times before I pick up a phone and call. When avoiding fear is the 10, I lose. I no longer want fear to steal my precious time and attention, do you?

False 10s offer a wonderful cocktail of outsized promise (often relief of some sort), and a chase that helps focus me down (again offering relief). There is something wonderful about losing myself in something — *anything* — even if it is not what I really wanted to be doing. Every day, every minute offers me too many choices and I get overwhelmed. Everything comes to me at the same volume, which makes turning to the news for a dose of injustice a welcome distraction. Outrage is a wonderful way to focus.

I have begun the practice of looking at false 10s as if they are any deadly addiction. I think through the drink, when I remember I need to. The moment I can pause and get conscious of what I am chasing, I am at the point of choice. It takes practice, practice practice, but eventually, when the bell rings, we don't have to answer it.

Believe me, I have shopped for and bought new cars, just to have a compelling project rather than face the mundane of every day life. If I can spot a false 10, you can. I have had the same car for over 2 years now. Given one of my favorite false 10 habit of trading in my car yearly, I would say, something must be working.

I am not a victim of the world's priorities and interruptions. Every day is a minefield of false 10s, choices and prioritizing. We are asked to lead the PTA, our kid gets sick, a fun opportunity comes along, or a compelling "emergency" crops up at work. It can feel like an endless feeling of "my life is not my own," and "I have no choices." But it's not true. It takes work and practice, but over time, how we see things can shift. When our view of those things finally shifts, the world changes. Gandhi wasn't wrong.

I go through a process with everything that comes into my world. What started as a painful and deliberate exercise, while I was learning, has become a simple, 30-second contemplation. Sometimes I am presented with a hard choice or dilemma, and I still need to write it out or talk with someone. Writing it out, or talking it out, helps me figure out if something I want to do, but feels suspect, will really bring me the outcome I think I am seeking. It is a good way to ferret out a false 10.

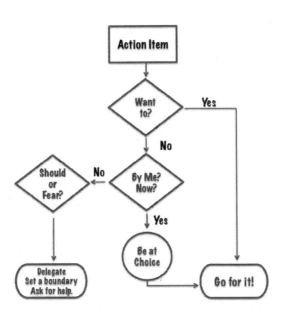

Let's take an everyday interruption that can derail a well-planned day. My child has a sore throat. They really *should*

go to the doctor and get a strep test. We have ourselves a very compelling, "should."

Clearly, I do not want to do it. I'm busy! I have a meeting, a project due, an unsympathetic boss. But it needs to be done (now), and I am the only one around.

Am I a victim? Once I get the initial grumble of annoyance out, or deal with the fear of what this means for my day, I can pause and take back my life. This may seem like a small distinction, but this simple exercise can change my whole day, my mood and how I treat my own sick kid. Bigger choices will come down the pike with the same dynamic, making this good practice. Practice, Practice, Practice.

So, how do I move from a victim of circumstance to the owner of my time and attention? Find the 10 and choose. I am a father. I love my kid. I want my kid healthy. I want to care for my kid. I will take him to the doctor, because caring for my kid is a 10. Of course it is. That extra 30 seconds changes everything. It forms a habit in the way I see my world, and the way things come at me. *I chose.* I can choose not to take the kid to the doctor, or I can choose to wait until tomorrow, but then I did not care for our kid in the way I believed necessary. Do I really want to make an annoying boss a 10 above the well being of my family members? I always get to choose.

It takes work to eat a salad instead of a piece of pizza, but over time, it changes everything.
False 10s are our enemies. Find them. Be ruthless. Guard

the only resources you ever truly own, *your time and your attention*. Yes, it takes work. And practice, and resolve, and commitment. To your 10s...and your life.

I don't want to do it, but it needs to be done!
In his amazing book, *Relax Into Wealth*, Alan Cohen has a chapter titled, "If it's not fun, hire it done." There are so many tasks I hate to do, I am not very good at, or I really do not have real time to do. Often, someone else can breeze through them in an hour where it would take me four, not counting the time to get ready to take on the task, walk around the task, and finally force my way through the task.

As a salesman, I racked up a large amount of expenses each week while entertaining clients, traveling, etc. The money came directly out of my wallet until I submitted the request for reimbursement, and the company paid. The charges averaged $2,000 per month of real, cash money. Most of my employers had rules (some would bend, some would not) of getting the expense report submitted within 60 days (some policies were shorter).

When I submitted six months of expenses twice a year (often over $10K), I would get some serious and understandable blow-back, because that was undermining the operational integrity of the finance group. The admonishment from my management was small compared to the agony of finding receipts, remembering appointments, mileage or meals well after the fact, and wondering how much money I had ultimately lost just because I couldn't find or remember an expense long after it was incurred.

My admin offered her help. "Mark, send me your receipts and mileage each week, and I'll submit your expenses for 10%."

So here I have a choice. Averaging $20K a year of expenses at 10% is $2,000. That is a lot of money. But wait, let's do a pragmatic cost analysis of this offer.

Reporting some six months of expenses took me approximately 6-8 hours each time. I made an average of about $500 per hour when I was working on revenue-producing work. That meant just the act of creating expense reports was costing me $500 X 6 = $3,000 in opportunity cost. I also dropped out at least 10% if not more of my expenses, due to inattention and disorganization, another $2,000.

My admin, in contrast, was a master of spreadsheets, it took her a quarter of the time to complete the task, and she loved the extra "found" spending money from taking on a little side job. In turn, she loved me, too! Remember, I had agonized over every element of the process, made mistakes, and got grief constantly. Plus it was on my "to do" list every week, causing me guilt and stress whether I did the task — or worse, let it go.

So let's see.....
6 Months Expenses.................. 6-8 Hours

I make Approx. $500/hr.......... $500*6 = Opportunity Cost of $3,000

I dropped out at least 10% anyway..........Another $2,000

Admin takes 1/3 of the time, no mistakes, likes doing it, LOVES the $$

I agonized over the process, unfinished task on my to do list every week and got a ton of grief for not getting it done.

No brainer for me!

Human nature (or at least, mine) will minimize the pain at first when confronting the dollar amount to be paid out to delegate or admit we need help. I will discount the opportunity cost, because I can always do it on the weekend, or over two evenings. If you can do it, will do it, and the savings is worth it — go for it. If your reality is more like mine, Earnest doesn't always do what he thinks he will do. And he gets us into lots of trouble.

Ultimately, I took her up on her offer because of the pain factor alone. It was worth it to me. In hindsight, and the more I do *this* work, I see even more benefits to "hiring it out." I have ever since.

This entire book is set to beat back Earnest, stop pushing my way through everything, and find some breathing room. When I get breathing room, I can make choices that improve every area of my life.

I let go of what I am not good at, which gives me time to do what I *am* good at. I get more bang for my buck (or my time). I let go of that familiar vice grip of "should, have to, and dread," leaving me room to have a productive thought (or lots of them) instead.

I create opportunity and relationship with other people whose strengths complement mine. And I don't have to submit my #*(% expenses, *ever*!

"But shit has to get done, whether I want to do it or not!" I hear you. I hear it in my own head. Yes, shit needs to get done. But questions to ask are, "Does it really?" And also, "By whom, and by when?"

I painted my office to save the money. Earnest thought it would be easy. It took me three days, and I did a pretty good job. My handyman painted my entire basement in one day, and it is perfect. I'm never painting a room again. In fact, my handyman can build a wall unit, fix a ceiling fan, and replace a toilet. Only I can write my book, coach my clients, and enjoy my kid's baseball game.

Hire it out.

Delegate.

Take the consequences consciously.

Or make it a 10.

You are NEVER a victim. You always have choice.

FEAR

Fear is such a huge factor in my day-to-day actions that it deserves its own chapter. Fear causes global chaos, war, political vitriol, divorce, and all sorts of nastiness in the world. Fear sucks!

Everyone wants to dance, the wallflowers want to dance, they are just afraid.
I have no idea who said that everyone wants to dance, but when I read it, I was busted. My ex-wife loves to dance, and would be the first one on the dance floor, no matter the situation. When I drank, I danced all the time. Sober, I only danced when 8 or more people preceded me. I wanted to dance, it looked like fun, but I couldn't step out. *Until...6...7...8...now I can dance. Pppphhheewww!*

I want to dance, sing, draw. I want to play softball, stand on stage, write a blog. To say I don't is bullshit. It's hiding behind fear. Admitting that I want to do so many things is the first step. Dealing with the fear, and getting past it is the last.

People asked me to speak on creating wealth.

"Mark, would you share how you made so much money? How could we be like you?"

"That's easy. I'm terrified every day, I have no self esteem, I'm not cool. One day I realized I am never not going to be terrified, I will probably never have self esteem, and no matter how hard I try, I will never be cool. I get up and show up anyway. That's it."

When I got my first sales job at a high tech start up, I woke up terrified every day. I would steel myself for a day of being so far out of my comfort zone that I couldn't see dry land. In hindsight, my 10 was an opportunity to provide for my family, and the fear was a 9.9. One day, I had a realization that reframed that fear and changed my beliefs about being fearful.

I remembered being a waiter at the Four Seasons hotel. I remembered how I felt at the beginning of every shift, as the rich and famous, the world leaders, and the self-important would be sitting in my section. I was terrified. I would literally sweat while I was polishing my silverware. I realized that I was always terrified — as a waiter, a student, on a date. It didn't matter the scope or the engagement, the fear was the same.

This high-end, intimidating job was no different. If I was terrified as a *waiter*, I might as well be terrified *and make a ton of money*.

When something is a 10, fear is not an issue. A 9.9, and fear wins! Fear loves to play 10. True 10s bump fear out of top billing.
Fear will look like resistance. Fear will look like confusion.

For me, it is the root of all indecision, of over analyzing, and behind the exhausting choices that feel like rolling a boulder up the hill. It will get me to say and believe things that are not true to avoid what I *really* want to do. When fear is a 10 and my want is a 9.9 or below, fear wins.

Conversely, when I want something so bad, that I blow past fear, I know it is a 10. I would fight a bear to protect my kids. There is a clue here.

Terror is one thing, but when fears are small and quiet, they are insidious and can place a fog between me and what would probably be a 10. That's where discernment comes in.

Fear of making the wrong choice. Fear of what people will think. Fear of losing out.
As I went through this process, and saw just how much these little fears dictated my choices and actions, I started to get angry. "I am not going to dance because of what the people sitting at the tables will think?" Really?

When I slow down and see the fear for what it is, again I am at *choice*. I still give in to them daily, in small and large ways. But now I see what it costs me. I now find it unacceptable for fear to keep me from using my time and attention for what I want in life. So I practice leaning in. I choose where to risk and experiment. Every time I chose to go past the fear and act, or speak, or chose, or say no, that muscle gets stronger. And my life gets bigger.

MY WEEKLY AND DAILY PRACTICES

Through practice and awareness, I earned my freedom and started the train of productivity rolling. Through trial and error, I found my white board, my journal and my calendar to be the three tools I need to keep focused on my 10s. I am no longer a fan of having a ton of lists to keep track of and keep updated. Instead, I have learned to trust that if something wants to be important, it will make itself known. However, that is a little too New Agey even for me, so I do write some items down. I keep track of my 10s on three small and focused lists.

Radar
Action items that will become a 10, but are not now.
Deadline or due date (should be put on calendar when date known)

The Week's 10s
Absolutely must be or wants to be done this week.
Once scheduled put on calendar.

Today's 10s
You really want to do it.
Deadline, due date or consequence if not done today.
Anything scheduled.

Radar

I use the radar for things that I know are important, are not a 10 this week, but I do not want to lose sight of altogether. The only criteria: I know they will be a 10 at some point. Many things can be scheduled, and if you are good with your calendar for non-meeting type prompts, I wholeheartedly support you using it. But for me, there are some things I am not ready to commit to, so I cannot schedule yet. I have done it before and blown them off. They are still important enough to become a 10, so I want to keep track of them until my attention makes them so, or a compelling event forces them onto a list.

Watch your radar. It is not a catchall for all the things you don't want to forget. Keep it short.

The dentist is the perfect radar item for me. I know I need to go, but I do not like to commit to an appointment six months in advance. If I put it on my calendar to schedule, I will push it — week after week. So it goes on my Radar the first week it comes up to my attention. I'd love to be the kind of person who schedules it the moment the alert comes up, but I am not. It has to be a 10, or I don't do it. Essential paperwork, follow up calls, an awesome idea I had for business but not pulling the trigger yet — these are all radar items. I generally update my radar once a week after I enter my current week 10s.

This Week's 10s

This is my radar for *this week*. I fill it in on Sunday night or Monday morning, and move items over to the daily list. I love using my white board, however, if you are more mobile, and it works for you, your journal or phone app are also good ways to track 10s. Personally, I want my list as a reminder, but I do not want it cluttering my day. I set it and forget it — mentality and physically. Much of the time, they are things I have resistance to, and therefore won't put on a calendar. Earnest would put it on the calendar, but I know better. For example, paying bills that are due, booking a trip, finally scheduling the dentist. I find it easier write it down unscheduled than the often advertised "plan your week" exercise. For some reason, writing down the 10s for the week, the things that I want to happen — or must happen with no specific commitment — also opens up my willingness to address the other things that must be done, *this week*, and *by me*, because of whatever 10 I have discovered about those tasks and actions. Remember, this is an experiment, but the goal is too keep you as free as possible.

Today's 10s

This is the only list that actually matters. Today is all I have, today is all I can deal with, and today is the only day I can actually do anything anyway. As I said, my time and attention are my only commodities, and because all things on my list and in my head have equal urgency, I make sure this list has a red velvet rope around it. Only the elite may enter. The 10s on "today's list" are exciting to me for any number of reasons, but they all hold do-or-die energy. If they made it to today's list, I have already found the reason that even the most mundane actions reward me.

Guard today like a junkyard dog. 9.9s and below get chased out.

9. 9's may creep into the week's list or the Radar, but they never make it to today's list. If they do, and they show themselves, get them off. The relief is amazing.

Working with the lists.

In this example, it's a Tuesday morning and I have set up my day. I love coming into my office after my workout and writing on my board. I sometimes do it the night before, but like I pack for a trip, it is as close to boarding time as possible. Almost always, a check mark goes next to Exercise and Meditate as I write the list, because they are 10s and are also usually done by this point in the day. It also gives me a feeling of satisfaction to check a couple of 10s off before confronting the rest of them.

Radar	The Week's 10s	Tuesday's 10s
Insurance Application (30th)	2 book chapters	Exercise
Dentist Appointment	Deposit to bank	Meditate
Call Pete Johnson	Client Invoices	John 8:30am
Return lamp	Pay bills	Rich 11 am
Meeting with Karen	Book CA trip	Zack Baseball 7pm
17 Lies books to clients.	Lunch - Mom	Mom Paperwork
Final Edits to Stacy	Guitar	Bob Invoice
Follow up Max, Julie, Rich	Schedule Chris	Guitar 1 2 3
	Zack Baseball Tue	Call Chris
	Mom Paperwork	
	Schedule Dentist	

If you look at my Radar, you will see an assortment of things: the paperwork I don't really want to do, but has a deadline; calls I really want to return; an idea I had for my clients, and prospective conversations, which I *want* to do; and other work that furthers my projects. Anything that I was able to schedule, I did, and that is no longer on my Radar. As I add items to my week or day's list, I cross them off the prior list. I decided this is the week to schedule a dentist appointment, so it made it to the list (notice, it's Tuesday and I still have not scheduled it, so you still see it on the week).

The Week's 10s are also inclusive of actions that fit the "10s" criteria but have no schedule. I always wait until the last minute to book trips. Last time it cost me $800 to wait though, and I want to save that money. It feels like a commitment, a trap I want to avoid, but I want that money more, so it made the list. I have no idea what day works to have lunch with my mother, but I know I want to do it, so it is on the week's list. The paperwork for my mother is daunting, and I don't want to do it, however the deadline is Wednesday and my 10 is avoiding the consequences. It is also on Tuesday's list (with Chris and Zack) so they are crossed off.

Tuesday is set now, with Appointments, the things I want to do, and the things I hate to do, or always avoid doing, but want done for whatever underlying reason or consequence that makes them a 10. Thanks to this practice and the freedom of my thinking, I can actually do those "not so fun tasks" without much drama these days. You will also notice that "Guitar" is on the week's list and the daily list. It is a 10 for me to learn the guitar, and I want to practice three times a day to attain a goal I have set for myself.

Radar	The Week's 10s	Wed 10s
Insurance Application (30th)	2 book chapters	✓Exercise
Dentist Appointment	Deposit to bank	✓Meditate
Call Pete Johnson	Client Invoices	✓Sarah 8:30 am
Return lamp	Pay bills	✓4PC 11 am
Meeting with Karen	Book CA trip	○Andy 3 pm
17 Lies books to clients.	Lunch – Mom	✓Send completed Paperwork
Final Edits to Stacy	Guitar	⬤Joe, Sarah Invoice
Follow up Max, Julie, Rich	Schedule Chris	⬤Pay Bills
	Zack Baseball Tue	○Bank
	Mom Paperwork	Guitar 1 2 3
	Schedule Dentist	⬤Date Night
		✓Call Dentist
		⬤Write

In this illustration, it's now 1:30pm Wednesday. The week's list is getting crossed off. There are items still on there, while some are in process, some I have resistance to, and some will get checked off at the end of the week when they get done.

In truth, I use lots of color on my white board, to make it fun and keep the practice from becoming monotonous. I'll spare you and only use two colors for consistency and my editor's sake, but I have 8 marker colors in reality. I can ignore important items in front of me if I want to, so using vivid color grabs my attention.

My morning appointments are checked off.

A few action items are checked off, and some have dots. I put a dot next to a task that I have done *some* work on, but is still waiting on either information or another action. I do this for a sense of momentum and satisfaction. The invoices are done, and just need to be sent. I have done 80% of my writing goal today. I paid some bills (the ones due tomorrow). Date night is scheduled.

The items with the circle are there to remind myself they are *still* there, and I have validated that they are *still* 10s. If I leave them blank, they get lost. The doughnut hole is my recommitment ceremony to a 10. By the time I shut down, the list gets acknowledged; I smile, and erase it. Sometimes I put the next day's list together, sometimes I don't.

What you don't see on the list is all the time I spent reading news, Facebook, looking at my fish, talking to friends on the phone, or generally not paying attention to my list. Some kind of strange time warp occurs. I still "waste" time, but with this consciousness, I snap back to what is deeply important more efficiently than I used to.

If you haven't guessed, I will be booking my CA trip late in the day on Friday, because I absolutely have to put it off as long as possible, but I feel so exhilarated by completing my lists now that I will do it just to prove it was a 10.

It is important to note here that the whiteboard works for me. I need a visual cue to focus. But only on Today's list. Radar, and the week, are not visible in my day and do not distract me anymore. Use whatever method works for you. Play with it, make it your own. This is not a system with rigid guide-lines. It is only an illustration of how I keep myself honest — first to myself, and therefore to everyone else.

YOUR TOOLBOX

This practice itself is not that difficult. Figure out what you want to do, and do it. Pretty simple. It's the obstacles life throws at you that will make the journey to taking back your time and attention more...interesting.

Freedom isn't free, as the saying goes. I'd love to tell you that the world, your boss and your loved ones will welcome your 10s with open arms and a supportive demeanor. It is not that they don't support you, it's that they have their own 10s, whether they are conscious of them or not. And we all fight for our own 10s. As I journeyed this road, I found myself in unfamiliar territory, running into situations I hadn't anticipated. I needed to pick up new tools along the way if I was to take back the reins of my life.

Courage

You will need courage on this journey. I do not know where or when your "stuff" will come up, but it will. It may be a tough conversation, setting a boundary, or simply saying out loud, "I want to do this." It is different for everyone.

For me, asking Earnest to leave the room, and not be the "nice guy" in every situation was like facing death every time. My stuff, not necessarily yours. Just know some resistance and obstacles will come up in some form. Then know, sword in hand, you can and will face your demons — and you are always at choice to move forward when and if you want to. You can choose to back down or move ahead. Be kind to yourself, but choose. Watch your choices, and see what those choices reap. Trial and error alone will propel you ahead. You *can't* fail.

Risk

I can promise very few things with this way of living, but I promise that you will need to accept risk. As with courage, I am not sure where, but at some point you will need to close your eyes and jump, and maybe not see where you'll land. It may be saying no to staying late at work, it may be showing your art for the first time, but it will feel like a risk. Go for it, or don't, but be aware of what each choice costs you or brings you.

Tough Conversations

Sometimes the only thing standing between me, and what I want, is a conversation I don't want to have. *I don't want to hurt someone's feelings, I am embarrassed, I think they will get angry, I'm being unreasonable.* These thoughts are examples of the ones that have preceded important conversations I have had. Sometimes it is only this scary chatter that stands between me — and my 10. It's fear, so I need to stop and decide which is going to get to be that 10.

No

It's true. "No" is a complete sentence. Use it. "Yes, but," is also a good default response to cultivate. "I will do this for you, but I need _____ in order to be able to accommodate your request," is a good way of making sure you are leveraging your time and attention in a way that works for you. Often, I do not know my answer right away, so my automatic response defaults to "yes" — and I often regret it later. It is ok to answer with a pause. I have gotten into the habit of answering, "I am not sure, give me a few minutes and I will call you back." Then I can do my inner work to decide the best answer for me.

Boundaries

Good fences make good neighbors. Clear boundaries make for good relationships. Boundaries are the antidote to resentments. 9 times out of 10, if I am angry, or carrying a resentment, it is because I didn't set a boundary. You know the people in your life who set boundaries. Chances are, if you have a hard time setting them, you judge them pretty harshly, at least at first — but I bet you respect them. The people you meet with the best boundaries are usually the ones living their 10s.

Love and Kindness

The point of all these decisions is to live a full life, filled with the activities and people that I love. When saying no, setting a boundary or having any tough conversation, love and kindness is always appropriate. It is the tool to ground all the others. The more I treat myself with love and kindness, the easier it is to allow myself to focus on my true 10s. There is a difference between self-care and "being selfish." Making sure that love and kindness are guiding principles for all concerned, including myself, ensures I can keep the *people* in my life a 10 while I also pursue what excites and inspires *me*.

For more on shoring up your toolbox, I highly recommend Steve Chandler's *Time Warrior*. Frankly, the journey would have been a tougher road without reading Steve's invaluable insights and suggestions.

TOUGH CONVERSATIONS

Every so often, our resistance to something that we *thought* was a 10 is trying to tell us something. The following story is an excerpt from a conversation I had with a colleague about the resistance I felt. The talk had me worked up about letting people down, but as you will see, having the courage to open up a conversation about it paid off.

"The Leadership Program, now that is also a 10. It is so cool, and I love working with Stacy. The website is up, the concept is right on the money and people seem to be excited about it."

"Has anyone signed up?"

"No but I am having great conversations. Again, they lead to more one on one type of ventures but they all think it is interesting. Stacy is having trouble with enrollment also. We have the message and it is right on target. But..."

"But what, Mark"

"F$#k! I really want to do it. But it is not like the book or my coaching business. Those are so clearly 10s. Oh no, this is like a 9.9. I'm excited, I love the idea. I love the idea of partnering with Stacy. It would be so cool. But there is something missing. I know a 10. Nothing will stop me when something is a 10. This isn't like that."

"Then you know what you need to do, Mark."

"Oh no, I can't call Stacy and pull out of this. I just can't. I committed. I hate this. I do not like to back out of things and I really hate disappointing people."

The feelings of fear and shame were kicking my butt. I had no idea what to do with this.

"What if you called her and were honest?"

"Ugh. Not sure I have the guts to do it. Wait, I can tell her the truth. I really love working with you, love the idea, but it's not a 10 for me, at least not yet. I'd like to talk to you about how to make it a 10. OK, that I can do."

When I did call Stacy and confessed my truth, she said "OMG, I am so with you. This isn't sticking at a 10 for me, either."

Well, that was unexpected.

Watch out for the 9.9s

The more I worked with this new insight, the more I learned about myself. I started to see more clearly the motivations under the desires. Some of those motivations were internal, some were not. The internal ones were clear. I was on fire. The external motivations were based in feelings like fear and shame, as we discussed previously. Earnest plays a big part in creating 9.9s. He falls for the belief that I "should" want to do something.

I looked back over my life. I thought of the things I have accomplished and the things I quit or have just never panned out. I started to see that anything that was a 10, for whatever reason, I did. If it wasn't a 10, I procrastinated, agonized over, beat myself over, and if it did get done, it was the day it became a 10 because of a deadline or a consequence I wanted to avoid.

Then it hit me.

I always do 10s. I struggle with everything else.
What if Stacy and I had never talked about this tiny reservation we each felt about that project? It wasn't even a well-formed thought at the time, just a feeling under the surface of something we were both initially excited to work on. Being honest brought it to the light, so we could figure out how to make this project a 10 — or agree to walk away.

In tough conversations, if we are truthful, we can always leave the relationship in a better place. Of course, we cannot control other people's reactions. More often than not, though, we are a tough, honest conversation away from feeling alive and free.

I keep a close watch on projects that get stuck in the mud. Whether it is my own resistance or outside forces, something is up. I can be excited and think I am all in — but those pesky 9.9s that Earnest gets me into are the life force killers.

Just because something looks cool, looks like the "universe" is dropping it into my lap, doesn't mean it really is for me to do. If I start to notice resentments, or a secret hope that the project goes away, I am getting clues. I will go down a wrong road with enthusiasm and excitement, but I need to be willing to cut the cord as soon as I get clear *it ain't* a 10!

WHEN MOM CAME TO TOWN

This book almost didn't come into being. I committed to a launch date, chose an editor and a publisher, told everyone in the world that I was writing it — and started. Awesome concepts hit the page, my life and business were firing on all cylinders, I was astounded at how my A.D.D. magically disappeared, and my to-do lists were vanquished — one after the other.

I was scheduled to give a 10-minute talk in front of my peers touting the discovery of how living the "Only 10s" life had been a *miracle*. I couldn't wait. Then...two weeks before the presentation...my 83 year old mother comes to town.

I actually had it all planned out. My mother could no longer live on her own in Florida, and needed to be in assisted living. I found an amazing place a few miles from my house, and it all seemed to be falling into place. Did I mention, *I had this all planned out*?

I had no doubt the plans and systems I had in place were going to make this work, like clockwork. I am great at setting boundaries, hiring help, delegating, and saying no. I live the principles in this book so well that I even hired an eldercare transition expert, to help my mother sort through her stuff, unpack, set up her apartment and move in. *I so got this.*

The day my mother moved in, the director of the facility mentioned something called "Transition Trauma." She said it happens to everyone, it is unavoidable, and it will pass. I scoffed at her prediction. I meditate. I set boundaries. I hire help. I am writing a book on all of this. *Please! I got this.*

The moving truck breaks down, and is going to be a week late. My mother is coming with so much stuff that the facility will not allow delivery, so it will all need to go into...*my garage*. My transition expert had a vacation planned, and now the delayed truck was coming the day after she leaves. My mother calls five times a day in a panic. She has debilitating arthritis, and every action is difficult and painful. She is in a new place, without the essentials that help her get along (they are all on the truck), and more importantly, there is no HBO.

Cue the narration; see both Mark and his alter ego Earnest making daily trips to Chesterfield Residences by this point. We go to Wal-Mart, Target, and Bed Bath and Beyond for desperately needed supplies. Baseball games, tutors and regular parental duties were strained, but never fell off our list. Earnest has shown up, and he can always run faster, do more and be everything to everyone. *Relax, I still got this.*

A couple of days into the move, we all get sick. I mean really sick. The coughing, the chest pain, and weakness hits us like a ton of bricks. My mother, already weak and unsteady, is unable to care for herself. Not only are Earnest and I handling things heroically, we are doing so with a headwind. I hate to admit it but I am starting to crack. *I am not so sure I got this.*

Transition trauma. And it is as bad as they warned.

I am in hell. I do not have this. Resentments are everywhere. I am exhausted and feel like crap. I am sure I made the biggest mistake of my life. My mother is miserable and looking like she is going to die. We fight every day. I say things I can never take back. I want to burn all her belongings still in my garage. Boundaries are gasping for air. Fears flying. "Shoulds" are a way of life. I have failed.

And... what the hell am I going to talk about when I do this presentation? How the hell can I write a book when I hate every minute of my life? I am really a failure.

Soon, it's time for my business trip, and I am thankful for the break. My mother is miserable but stable. The Transition Expert will be back from vacation, and ready to start dealing with my overflowing garage. My natural remedies are holding this crud to a manageable nuisance so I can function. I leave for Los Angeles to give my presentation on "10s, Boundaries, Tough Conversations etc." I admit, by the time I left I was wondering what I was going to talk about now? I am definitely did not see myself as the poster boy for my own concept.

Panic fully set in as my presentation neared. I had made this discovery, I was on fire, getting things done, creating like mad, setting boundaries, and simplifying my life. But since my mother arrived, I hadn't done a thing on my own 10 list! I was exhausted, and moreover, embarrassed. I am a fraud and I have nothing to share.

Then, through prayer, meditation and journaling, it dawned on me.

My mother was the 10. Of course she was. Being a stand up guy and a good son is a 10.
She was sick, scared, disoriented, and things needed to be taken care of *now,* and *by me*. She was the very definition of a 10. I had delegated and hired out all I could, but some things were just going to have to be me. I didn't *want* to do all these things, but I *did* want to be a good son and a responsible adult. I wanted my 83-year-old mom to be comfortable and cared for. I could choose this instead of being a victim.

Ironically, I was doing my 10 all along, but I was fighting it. Being a victim instead of choosing it and owning it. It was indeed appropriate to put other 10s aside, *for now.* My business trip was also a 10, so when the time came, I got on the plane and trusted things would be handled while I was gone.

"And then my mother came to town," was the line to get the biggest laugh of my presentation. Of course, everyone could relate. We are high achieving, kick-ass people who set our lives up the way we want them, and then, sometimes life just comes crashing in. And we all have family, emergencies, and life circumstances that are out of our control.

My mother coming to town made my presentation, and this book, even better.
It is awesome to work on 10s every day. I love creating my life and choosing where my to focus my attention. But, it is when life comes calling in unexpected and overwhelming ways; practices developed during calmer times truly come into necessity.

I learned many lessons from this time with my mother.

Sometimes the people I love just need me, and my time and energy. Loving is a 10.
And sometimes it just has to be me who provides the care. Knowing the kind of person I want to be, who I choose to be, makes the 10 easy to spot. When an emergency happens, I can confidently clear the decks, allow it to be a 10 — and dive in.

Just because I can, doesn't mean I should.

At some point, Earnest needs to go, and I need to take care of myself. There are times and situations that become bottomless pits of need. No matter how much I give, it will not be enough. I can say no, even if I am capable of doing something, and allow someone else, that person, or nobody to step up. I think of Oscar Schindler at the end of the movie. "This ring could have saved 25 more people." My inner Schindler will always feel guilty and that I could have done more.

Boundaries, priorities and the reins need to come back.

At some point, much sooner than Earnest would allow, it's done. My life, my 10s, my priorities come back into play. Maybe little by little, but they come back. People may get annoyed, disappointed, and still need, but they are more resourceful than it looks or they think. Put the white horse away and let them be their own hero.

I can choose in any situation.

Much of the pain of this experience came from my resistance. I fell into victim role quickly, and forgot that I had a choice. I may not like the choices, but I still get to choose. Even when I only chose the path I *hate the least*, the choosing is empowering. I get energy from knowing I decided to do it.

Sometimes it just sucks.

Sometimes there is nothing I can do. If I am a caring, open

person, life is going to get messy. Find joy, humor and relationship where I can. Everything passes.

And yes, it's all a gift.

I am a better person, and this is a better book, because of "Transition Trauma." It dug up all kinds of childhoo patterns that I got the opportunity to work through. Quickly! We healed old wounds. My mother went through her own process, and is figuring out that she is responsible for her own well-being and happiness.

FINDING THE INNER COMPASS

"Mark, if I were in a foxhole, surrounded by the enemy, I would want you by my side. I know that you would get us all out to safety, without question. But if I were headed into a peacekeeping mission, I would leave you at home. I'm not sure you are done with the addiction to excitement. That is why I am not sure I want to work with you."

This was my first conversation with my coach, Rich Litvin. What a blow. I thought of myself as a new age, peace loving, man who would like nothing better than building new housing for homeless refugees, *on a peacekeeping mission.* But I knew he was right. I would build two houses and be off doing something else more interesting. I love the fight, I love shiny objects, I love the juice.

The truth was, my compass was broken. My day consisted of the search for a dopamine rush or, if I was hunkering down to accomplish something important, waiting for something shiny to walk by so I could accidentally get that rush. If my project weren't providing the interest, a friend in a crisis would do the trick. And hey, I was helping someone.

Ritalin helped. But only if I sat myself down, decided what to do, and got to work. If I didn't have a plan, I just focused harder on Facebook. I had to steer the ship in the direction I wanted *before* I took the pill. Especially, if what I was starting was mundane. If it was interesting, but frustrating, I would bounce off the second something else could distract me.

This brings me back to the conversation with Rich about following my energy. My fear was that I would follow this A.D.D. excitement junkie part of myself over a cliff, because the view was cool. In reality, something different showed up.

Instead of beating myself up for not *wanting* to do something that seemed important, I paid attention. Instead of doing something I didn't want to do, I asked more questions.

Why am I doing this? Why am I not doing this? What is really going on?
In the weeks after our conversation, I unpacked every action item that came my way. I did the same for my clients. I would go through our "to-do" lists and ask questions. We would get mindful of what was behind every demand on our time and attention. Something cool was happening to my clients and me.

The more conscious we are about the "Why" of our actions, the more we see choice.

With choice comes freedom. More often than not, the task itself held very little charge. It was the underlying fears and beliefs about those tasks that held all the information. The 10s in each situation started to reveal themselves.

I would rather do this than have a difficult conversation.

I would rather lie to myself than admit that I am afraid.

I would rather make them think better of me than say no.

I would rather avoid fear than speak, act, choose, or risk.

On and on, the underlying motivations clouded what I really thought about any given request or my own wants. It was a magnetic storm that messed with my compass.

"Mark, I am so stressed this week. We are overwhelmed with projects and I am short staffed. The CEO wants it done by Friday, and I just can't do it. I need to quit, I've had it with this stress and unrealistic expectations."

"What needs to happen to relieve your stress so you don't just quit?"

"I don't know."

"What would you do if you were bold, fearless, and willing to risk looking bad?"

"That's easy, I would have a conversation with the CEO to

adjust expectations or get more resources. Oh, I see where you are going..."

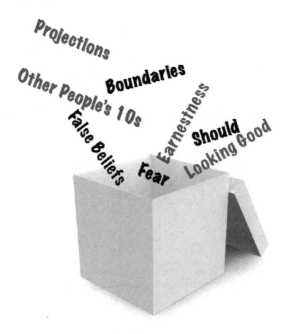

Unpacking and examining each item on my to-do list takes work. In fact, it is stressful and time consuming, *at first*. After a few days, it gets easier and I can make choices. Once I see the fear, the "shoulds," and the projection, I get clear on the right action. I may take on a task to avoid a consequence, but at least I know why I am doing it and choose. I am no longer "confused."

The same became true for the shiny objects. I want a fish tank. My koi pond is full, and I am banned from buying more fish. I go by the pet shop and look at the miniature sharks, and I can see the tank in my office. We have already established that I generally do what I want, and buy what I want, when I want it. But focusing on only 10s has ruined much of my random dopamine chasing. The fish tank is an 8. Distracting myself from the work of the three projects I say are 10s is a 9. The projects are, in fact, the 10s. The fish tank doesn't fit. The time and attention it consumes will take me away from what is really important to me. I grumble, but I choose.

Same with my car. I recently traded in my convertible for a very luxurious, and awesome, small SUV. Best car I have ever owned. *But a convertible, that sounds great... the sun is out... Oh wait, I have a dog. I can go to Home Depot and throw stuff in my little truck. I blazed through the snow this winter.* Shiny object (convertible) is now seen for what it is.

Apple watch! I want one, gotta have one. I will look so cool. Oh wait, my wrist buzzing every 30 seconds. I'll also need to charge it, set it up, and pay attention to it. Yup, just a distraction.

This is how I find my compass every time it gets lost. The more I use my "to-do" list as a practice in why I am spending my precious time and attention on anything, the clearer I see where my compass is pointing. The more I slow down and look at my "impulses," I can see what I am really wanting.

So yes, you *should* have me in your foxholes. And yes, now I can go on that peacekeeping mission, too. I will build a house or two and love every minute. But then I will need to create something else compelling on the mission. By finding my inner compass, I no longer need to artificially create excitement (war). My compass knows what will be exciting, juicy, fun, awesome, and *worthwhile*.

FINDING TRUE NORTH, THE ULTIMATE 10

When it comes to 10s, trusting my attention and my enthusiasm became essential for daily momentum. As I teased out the false 10s and learned to zero in on my inner compass, I started getting things done at a rate I have never experienced. Now that I was freed, my mind went back to the big projects, goals and dreams I had discounted because of "A.D.D." and not trusting myself to follow through.

The energy that was tied up in fear and hypervigilance was released for creative and generative thinking. No longer beholden to beliefs that are not true, my white board filled with new ventures to pursue.

Then I thought of the Mark Zuckerberg "One Goal" story. What was my one goal? I had no idea. Whenever I want to figure something out, I head to the white board. I have an entire wall covered with enough whiteboard real estate to spread out and let my mind wander in all directions. My clients are also thrilled with the added space.

I wrote down my current projects and started asking questions of myself.

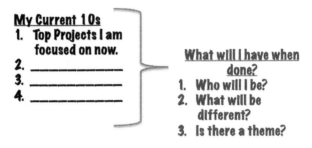

So when I actually accomplish these 10s, what does that mean? More importantly, how will life be different, how will I be different? What is the thread that ties them together?

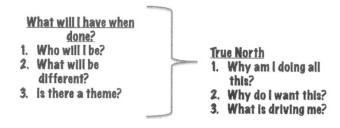

Like any good coach, I keep asking myself questions. My favorite question is a simple, "So?" That's shorthand for questions like, *So what? Why do I want to be this person, have this outcome, what is driving me? What is the deeper 10?* Now I am getting somewhere. The projects feed into my feeling a certain way, looking a certain way, or having some thing I want. Once I feel this or have that, is that the end? What do I ultimately want?

If we work backward, Mark Zuckerberg's one goal was to "Grow Facebook." Why? What was his true north? I have no idea why his one goal is to grow Facebook, but something is driving it. Let's go back to our original list of projects.

My Current 10s
1. Top Projects I am focused on now.
2. _____
3. _____
4. _____

Why are they 10s?
1. Do each fit in the context of True North?
2. For each, are they on purpose?
3. Are they really 10s?

Now that we know that we have more clarity on our motives, what we want, and how that leads to our "Ultimate 10" or Goal, we can question our projects individually. *Why* are they a 10? Sometimes one or two are on the list because we *want* to do them. If they excite me, and deemed not a distraction, then they stay and I continue questioning the list. Do these projects fit into the context of what I actually want for my life? Is it a 10...or is it an 8 or 9 side trip taking me off of my True North? If they pass the questioning, they stay. If not, they come off the list. I still may do them, that is not the point. If a new hobby, say, skydiving, is on the list but does not fit, we can still go skydiving. If it is a 10, it will end up being scheduled all by itself. But it is not something to keep front and center, because we have our eye on the ultimate prize.

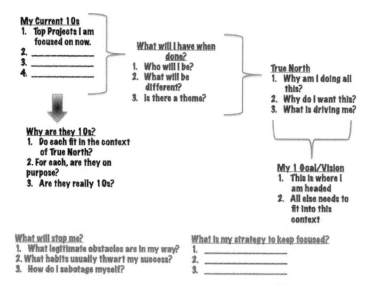

My Current 10s
1. Top Projects I am focused on now.
2. _____
3. _____
4. _____

What will I have when done?
1. Who will I be?
2. What will be different?
3. Is there a theme?

True North
1. Why am I doing all this?
2. Why do I want this?
3. What is driving me?

Why are they 10s?
1. Do each fit in the context of True North?
2. For each, are they on purpose?
3. Are they really 10s?

My 1 Goal/Vision
1. This is where I am headed
2. All else needs to fit into this context

What will stop me?
1. What legitimate obstacles are in my way?
2. What habits usually thwart my success?
3. How do I sabotage myself?

What is my strategy to keep focused?
1. _____
2. _____
3. _____

Let's look at the whole. The beauty of this exercise is that I can talk a client through from any section, and expand outward. They may know their ultimate goal, to build a company. We can work backwards to create projects that will support that outcome. Along the way, we will shore up his why and his drive to do so, drowning out any distractions.

After I questioned my projects, my motives and found my ultimate goal, I was curious as to what would stop me. I know my shortcomings well, so I list them out. Then I ask, how will I keep *these* from becoming a problem? I anticipate the stumbling blocks, and create strategies for staying on track in spite of them.

My clients find the exercise invaluable and simple. Get out a piece of paper or go to your own whiteboard, and start answering the questions and let yourself wander through your own mind. A mere 15 to 30 minutes later, you will be amazed at the insights.

For me, the easily distracted, having a bright intense star to shoot for is the best anti-glare tool for the myriad shiny objects that call from the side of the road.

RESISTANCE AND THE 10

I am sitting here with my heart in my mouth, and my brain all a fog. I want to go to Facebook, the news, eat something, or find anything at all to do besides write this chapter. It's painful, and I hate this feeling. Maybe this isn't a 10. Maybe I'm a fraud.

Stephen Pressfield would call it "resistance" in his masterpiece, *The War of Art.*

My psychiatrist would call it A.D.D.

My enneagram type says it is part of my personality. We "sevens" feel "trapped" by any task or commitment.

All I know is that I am battling between something I really want to do, and wanting to relieve this tight anxious feeling at any cost. It has been a 50-year battle to date. I've been very successful in business and life. However, I have also made my way through school, jobs, and almost anything I need to do through using shortcuts and hacks. But only when the stakes are high enough. If the stakes are not high enough, I walk away. It was a creative way to live, and to navigate the shortcomings of my "personality," but it left me fatigued by the daily battle.

How many things have I started only to walk away? How many things sit half done? How many ideas pop into my head that excite me only to fade as fast as they showed? I've had enough, I no longer live this way. I will sit at this keyboard until something happens. I will type crap, but I will type.

It's been 20 minutes. I started by bouncing around the pages like a beach ball, writing and rewriting random paragraphs — and now I am finishing a chapter. The lump is gone. I am flowing. I feel like I took a Ritalin, but I haven't. I have a meeting in 30 minutes that I wish weren't scheduled now, because I want to keep working. This is awesome, but how did it happen?

The desire to write this book outweighed the feelings by just enough to keep me going. Writing was a 10, so avoiding those feelings dropped to a 9. Like any muscle or habit, I am learning to work through the feelings and fog. But only because writing this book is a 10.

Resistance is real, it's painful, but it is no match for a 10. I have a confession to make. I used much of what I write about in this book to actually write this book. I am working on a big visible project for next month, my mother calls several times a day, we are readying my son for college, my website needs updating, I need to change my insurance, and they all want my attention. But most of these tasks are not on my Summer 2015 10 List.

Summer 10s
Finish iCoach Book
Only 10's book
PC Intensive Project

You will notice only three items are on this list. Although the other items I listed are important and take up quite a bit of my time and attention, they will happen automatically. I can trust that they will make themselves 10s on their own each week. My three projects will not. I need to carve out time to sustain them. Set boundaries. Work through obstacles, resistance and failure to bring them into reality.

If you are reading this book, you know it was a real 10 for me. You will also know that fear, resistance, tough conversations and everything else that might have stopped this book from coming into reality, were pushed from the top spot.

In my life, a 10 is the Royal Flush that beats any hand. Walking through resistance has been a practice for me. Leaning into fear, allowing myself to be uncomfortable, and walking through the dreaded fog is worse than going to the gym at 6:00 AM. But, because I want to fit into my Hugo Boss fitted shirts, I go. Because I want my life, I am willing to do the work on *these* muscles as well.

A CLIENT STORY

One of my clients, who also suffers from A.D.D. and an attraction to all things music and art, worked diligently to fit into the corporate world. Now a successful vice president of business development at a leading marketing agency, he couldn't shut off his passions that didn't seem to align with his day-to-day responsibilities. Exploring his list of current projects, and the projects he longed to work on, he showed clear energy in several directions that (at first) didn't fit into his job description. As he learned to trust his internal compass, he found creative ways to not only bring his love of music into his corporate world, but to do so in a way that would differentiate his firm.

I often dreamed about a career in the music business, but chose the marketing and ad agency route instead. Though I dabbled in music, I was never really able to create a way to satisfy my passion for the arts. I was good at my job, successful and making money, but something was missing.

Many years later, I found myself in a unique position to build a bridge between these two worlds by developing a platform that celebrates collaboration between brand marketers and the music business. It turned out their interests were increasingly aligning, and many of them didn't know how to capitalize. My vision was to develop an event series that would tour the country, bringing these interests together for a combination of networking, panels and industry learning, and live music performances.

My mind said it would be too difficult finding venues in every city, nobody would show up, someone else must be doing this already, my colleagues will wonder if this is a good use of my time and whether it aligned with the company goals.

Despite all the questions and insecurities, I knew I was on to something unique. There was a need in the market. It was unquestionably my passion, my 10, and I knew I was the one to create it.

I sold the vision to the executive team at my company and got to work.

The tour is off to a great start and the response has been more enthusiastic than anticipated. I learned that once I commit to something I completely and passionately believe in, things begin to fall into place.

I took a risk and followed where my energy and enthusiasm took me, and the result has opened up my career, a differentiation for my company, and brought my greatest passion into the mix.

Too often, the people who come to me for coaching have put themselves into a box that they think will keep them safe. They follow the rules, and they make themselves into the people they think they need to be to "get ahead." To do this they must shut off a piece of themselves, the very part that makes them creative, unique and energized. Of course it is risky to color outside the lines, to speak up, to offer outrageous ideas, but those are the ones that leap frog incremental success. Those are the ideas that give a company lifeblood to become more then they thought possible.

QUESTIONS, STATEMENTS, ANSWERS

So what about all the little stuff, the 3's, 4's, and 5's?
They all go. They all get off the list. Your "10" list, that is.
If a 4 or 5 crops up and you really want to do it, then it
becomes a 10. If you easily drop it out, it was never important. You do not have time or space for these things. If they
were that important or that fun, they would be a 10.

If it is a 3 today but you know it is going to be a 10 some
time in the future, it belongs on the calendar or the Radar
list instead. You can always do things that are less than a 10,
but only when they become a 10. Until then, keep them off
your visible list.

I have to go to work, even though I hate my job!
No, you don't. You want to eat. You want to support the people you love. You want health insurance. You do not *have* to go. But you do want what the job provides. Choose! Hate this job? What are you doing to get another one? You go to work because you do not want the consequences of not showing up more than you do not want to go. It still may suck, but you are not a victim here. Choose, change, act, but never allow yourself to be helpless.

I'll drop important stuff out!
No, you won't. If it is important it will make itself a 10, get itself scheduled, or goes on the "Radar List." If it doesn't make it to any of those places, it wasn't that important. If it becomes important, it will let you know. Trust yourself.

My lists are getting too long.
I love this one. I got so good at getting my lists done I put more and more on the list. Soon it was a to-do list, and my 10 was the satisfaction, at the end of the day, of seeing all those check marks. But that didn't last long. I have no passion for completed lists. It is easy to reset. When the list starts looking long and uninspiring, I take a break, go through the process and ruthlessly cut it down.

I have obligations, I have no time for my own 10s.
We all have obligations pulling at us. I have two sons and an aged mother to care for. I have bills to pay, and retirement

to save for. The question is whether they own the strings to my arms, legs and mind...or do I? It takes courage to look honestly at where I am allowing circumstance to dictate my priorities or my feelings. It takes courage to set a boundary, and take time for myself. It takes *risk* to say no. It takes *worth* to put myself on the list.

A quick story I heard at a seminar, addressing the specific needs of overworked women, that I have applied to my own life (with great difficulty at first). It has paid off in unexpected ways.

Women often give and give until their teacup is empty. Then they try and steal a little time to fill the cup again. Over and over, they give to their families and jobs from an empty cup. We suggest a better strategy, fill the cup first. Fill it until it is overflowing, and give from the saucer, the overflow. When you give from this place, it is abundant and loving, and infinite.

I am a better father when I take time to go to the gym or take Tuesday nights for my men's group. I am a better father when I have my own projects and passions. I show my kids, by example, how to be a full, happy adult. My spouse finds me more attractive, because I am interesting and alive. Of course, I do not do these things at their "expense." But I do tell the truth to myself, let go of Earnest, and find a more balanced approach. I was shocked to find out my kids are fine if I only go to half their baseball games.

A CALL TO ACTION

When my clients, who often seem to "have it all," break character and get honest about their lives, there seems to be a common experience. They all seem to long for something that feels lost. They are sheepish to admit that they want something more and are embarrassed to be "ungrateful" for all the blessings in their lives.

I have it all, it is selfish to want more.
I don't think it is *more* they want at all. It is easy to cut away false ambition driven by false beliefs of fear, but not so easy to face what is left. But, I often find that the things they are looking for are what is hidden in "what's left."

If I am not striving, proving myself, keeping up an image, what is left?
I think the hardest thing of all, in modern society, is to let go of all the marketing, the "shoulds," and the fears of being

left out. It's frightening to stop the noise to ask: "Who am I, and what do I want?" The first time I ask a new client, the answer is always "less stress or pressure." Always. But as we unpack, it becomes clear that most of the pressure is indeed self-made. Yes there are responsibilities and demands on us, but the stress part is optional. It is not easy to let go of being a victim (or outrage) to see my own part in creating what I *don't* want, but it is the only way forward.

Just because you don't want to see it, doesn't mean it isn't true.

We are the authors of our lives. There are scenes and characters that populate this world, but we wrote many of them with our past choices. Yes, unexpected obstacles or fortunes may come our way, but for the most part, if we look back, we can see what led us to exactly where we are at this moment.

And a great deal of it was the choices we made — or didn't make.

My challenge is simple, are you willing to put the work in to find out what you want? Are you willing to strip away the facade that masks who you are? Are you willing to matter, *really matter*? To put yourself on your own list?

How often have we learned that an ounce of discomfort now, will relieve a pound of pain later? I can promise you, though uncomfortable at times, the work is worth it.

All we own is our time and attention.

Our lives are built by daily choices about where we put our attention and how we spend our time. Simply looking at a to-do list, unpacking what is there for us to learn about ourselves, our joys, our avoidance and our patterns –and being willing to try anew — is a great place to start the journey.

This is a journey that for me, opened up a whole new world. Yes, I get my list done each day, and that is a miracle in and of itself, but I have received so much more from this simple exercise. Allowing only 10s in my life, trusting my real attention, and experimenting every day has exploded my business, enriched my relationships, given me endless energy and passion, and even gotten my taxes done on time.

If you would like more support on this journey, please visit me at: *http://www.markjsilverman.com/work-with-me.html* for more information on how to work with me.

In Gratitude,

Mark Silverman

ACKNOWLEDGEMENTS

A lifetime of friends, mentors and guides go into making a man who he is. I have been fortunate enough to have an unfair share of the world's gold standard.

ALAN COHEN

I read Relax into Wealth, and everything changed. We talked, and you said you "had a hunch about me," which put me on the path I have been searching for my entire life. I met you in Hawaii and found my heart and my home. Nothing in my life would be as it is if I hadn't met you, and I am head over heels in love with my life. Thank you.

RICH LITVIN

You have been the diamond cutter in my life. I brought 25 years of study, growth, and experience to our first conversation, and from that first connection you held the bar high. Sometimes so high, I couldn't even see it, but you were unwavering in your belief that it was barely a stretch for me. Your wisdom, example and love are invaluable to me finding my compass. Your silence my foil. You are easily the best among the great. P.S. Without that one provocative question, this book would not exist.

TOM MENDOZA

After I met you in Lanai, our mutual friend and colleague, Mike O. said, "The good news is, Tom Mendoza knows who you are. The bad news is, Tom Mendoza knows who you are, go sell something." It was never bad news. You are the leader I measure all others by. You taught me how to conduct myself in business with class and integrity and still win. I keep my "Top 10 Things I learned from Tom Mendoza List" on hand to share with others.

STAN BROMLEY

Stan, I was a 30-year-old waiter working my way through school (still). You took a chance on me and hired me into a professional position at the Four Seasons, even though I did not have the experience. It was the first time I had seen a fax machine (or worn a double breasted suit). You mentored me, believed in me, and showed me the first rungs on the ladder when I never even knew there was a ladder. Thank you, sir.

STEVE CHANDLER

I picked up Time Warrior and all my excuses went down like dominoes. We had one of the roughest conversations of my life, and it redoubled my resolve to succeed. I have read and listened to your wisdom so much that your voice is in my head daily helping me blow through any obstacle I momentarily think impossible. More importantly, your dedication to service in life and as a coach is my shining example of what is invaluable in this profession.

MICHAEL ANDERSON

You are gifted at what you do and without a doubt, one of the most sound and grounded men I have met in my travels. You helped turn absolute hell into a life I could not imagine. I am forever grateful. P.S. You can cancel the Ritalin prescription.

GREG COLLINS

From the day I opened the door that you and Mike slammed in my face, you have had my back. Outstanding positions, giant commission checks, and awards did not compare with knowing I had your respect in the most competitive game in town. You are one of a kind, and one of my favorite people walking the planet.

ABOUT THE
AUTHOR

Mark Silverman is a Force of Nature. When people spend time with him, they transform. Always. Some aren't ready for it. The rare ones are, and they want more.

They are ready for an Extraordinary Life.

They are ready for an Extraordinary Business.

They are ready for an Extraordinary Relationship.

Mark is not a coach or a consultant, although he has coaching and consulting clients alike. Every engagement is unique.

The common thread is a leap forward towards the intended result.

Mark is very human, very honest and very vulnerable. These qualities allow him to be real with his clients, and meet them on a deeper level than they are accustomed to, fostering long lasting, exponential results.

Mark has generated over $90 million in sales, and received numerous awards over his 15 year career at fast-moving, fast-growing companies like NetApp, VMware and EMC. He has led teams to work with CEOs, management and front line stakeholders to bring mutual success and close multi-million deals. His dedication to the success of all involved, through leadership, coaching, and mentorship was the training ground for his passion to support others to achieve their goals.

He has also stumbled. Mark has experienced failure at a few business ventures and relationships along the way, and knows the lows that come with living a full-out life. He is a master at turning a challenging situation into gold.

If you're ready for something truly extraordinary, if you have a challenge, a project or a goal that needs a little rocket fuel...or if you just know there is something more, but are not quite sure what it is, click on Mark's Work With Me Page and set up a free, deep coaching conversation. The only risk is getting what you want.

Contact Mark at www.markjsilverman.com

Difference Press offers solopreneurs, including life coaches, healers, consultants, and community leaders, a comprehensive solution to get their books written, published, and promoted. A boutique-style alternative to self-publishing, Difference Press boasts a fair and easy-to-understand profit structure, low-priced author copies, and author-friendly contract terms. Its founder, Dr. Angela Lauria, has been bringing to life the literary ventures of hundreds of authors-in-transformation since 1994.

YOUR DELICIOUS BOOK

Your Delicious Book is a trailblazing program for aspiring authors who want to create a non-fiction book that becomes a platform for growing their business or communicating their message to the world in a way that creates a difference in the lives of others.

In a market where hundreds of thousands books are published every year and never heard from again, all of The Author Incubator participants have bestsellers that are actively changing lives and making a difference. The program, supported by quarterly Difference Press book-marketing summits, has a proven track record of helping aspiring authors write books that matter. Our team will hold your hand from idea to impact, showing you how to write a book, what elements must be present in your book for it to deliver the results you need, and how to meet the needs of your readers. We give you all the editing, design, and technical support you need to ensure a high-quality book published to the Kindle platform. Plus, authors in the program are connected to a powerful community of authors-in-transformation and published bestselling authors.

TACKLING THE TECHNICAL ASPECTS OF PUBLISHING

The comprehensive coaching, editing, design, publishing, and marketing services offered by Difference Press mean that your book will be edited by a pro, designed by an experienced graphic artist, and published digitally and in print by publishing industry experts. We handle all of the technical aspects of your book's creation so you can spend more of your time focusing on your business.

APPLY TO WRITE WITH US

To submit an application to our acquisitions team visit
www.YourDeliciousBook.com.

*Confessions of an
Unlikely Runner:
A Guide to Racing
and Obstacle
Courses for the
Averagely Fit and
Halfway Dedicated*

by Dana L. Ayers

*Matter: How to
Find Meaningful
Work That's
Right for You and
Your Family*

by Caroline
Greene

*Reclaiming
Wholeness: Letting
Your Light Shine
Even If You're
Scared to Be Seen*

by Kimberlie
Chenoweth

*The Well-Crafted
Mom: How to
Make Time for
Yourself and Your
Creativity within
the Midst of
Motherhood*

by Kathleen
Harper

*Lifestyle Design for
a Champagne Life:
Find Out Why the
Law of Attraction
Isn't Working,
Learn the Secret to
Lifestyle Design,
and Create Your
Champagne Life*

by Cassie Parks

*No More Drama:
How to Make
Peace with Your
Defiant Kid*

by Lisa Cavallaro

*The Nurse
Practitioner's Bag:
Become a Healer,
Make a Difference,
and Create the
Career of Your
Dreams*

by Nancy Brook

*Farm Girl
Leaves Home:
An American
Narrative of
Inspiration and
Transformation*

by Margaret
Fletcher

Whoops! I Forgot to Achieve My Potential

by Maggie Huffman

Only 10s: Using Distraction to Get the Right Things Done

by Mark Silverman

The Inside Guide to MS: How to Survive a New Diagnosis When Your Whole Life Changes (And You Just Want to Go Home)

by Andrea Hanson

Lee & Me: What I Learned from Parenting a Child with Adverse Childhood Experiences

by Wendy Gauntner

The Peaceful Daughter's Guide to Separating from A Difficult Mother: Freeing Yourself From The Guilt, Anger, Resentment and Bitterness

by Karen C. L. Anderson

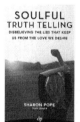

Soulful Truth Telling: Disbelieving the Lies That Keep Us From the Love We Desire

by Sharon Pope

Personal Finance That Doesn't Suck: A 5-step Guide to Quit Budgeting, Start Wealth Building and Get the Most from Your Money

by Mindy Crary

The Cancer Whisperer: How to Let Cancer Heal Your Life

by Sophie Sabbage

51335227R00068

Made in the USA
Lexington, KY
20 April 2016